Trient Press
3375 S Rainbow Blvd
#81710, SMB 13135
Las Vegas,NV 89180

Ordering Information:
Quantity sales. Special discounts are available on quantity purchases by corporations, associations, and others. For details, contact the publisher at the address above.
Orders by U.S. trade bookstores and wholesalers. Please contact Trient Press: Tel: (775) 996-3844; or visit www.trientpress.com.

Printed in the United States of America

Publisher's Cataloging-in-Publication data
Trient Press
A title of a book : Trientrepreneur

TRIENTREPRENEUR

ISSUE 13

Editor-in-Chief
Head Staff-Writer
Melisa Ruscsak

Managing Editor
Graphic Design Editor
Kristina Wenzl-Figueroa

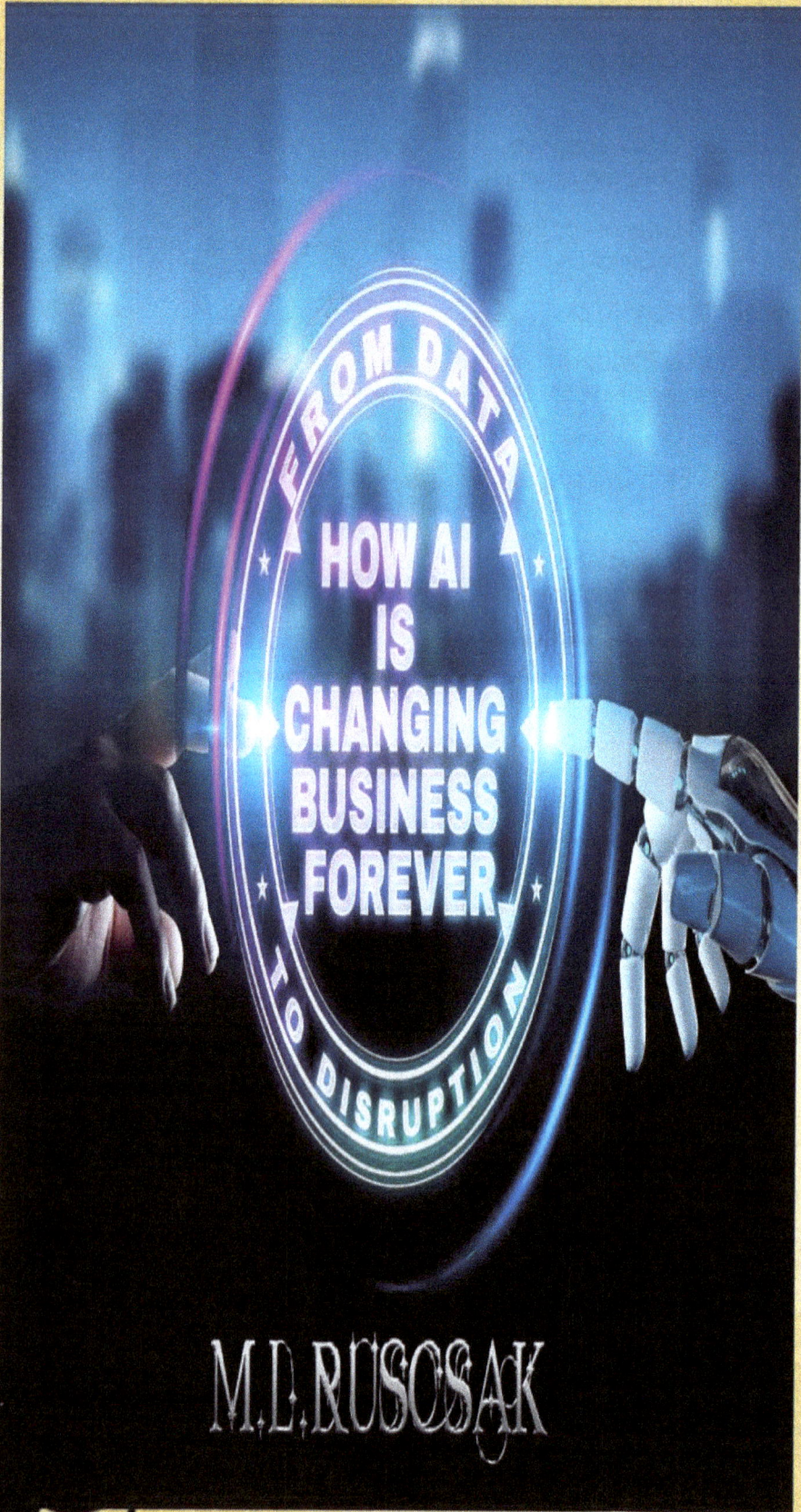

FROM DATA

HOW AI
IS
CHANGING
BUSINESS
FOREVER

TO DISRUPTION

M.D. RUSOSAK

Trient Press®

AUGUST/ SEPTEMBER AUTHOR TIPS

Author's Blueprint: Crafting a Powerful Brand for Writing Success.

- Define your author brand. Start by identifying the unique qualities and values that define you as an author. Consider your writing style, genre, themes, and target audience. This will serve as the foundation for your brand.
- Understand your target readers. Gain insights into your target audience's preferences, interests, and demographics. This knowledge will help you tailor your branding efforts to resonate with your ideal readership.
- Craft a compelling author bio. Your author bio should effectively communicate who you are as a writer and why readers should be interested in your work. Highlight your accomplishments, experiences, and the essence of your writing style.
- Develop a consistent online presence. Maintain a consistent and professional presence across your website, social media platforms, and other online channels. Use cohesive branding elements such as your author photo, logo, color scheme, and typography to create a unified brand image.
- Engage with your readers. Build a connection with your readers by actively engaging with them through social media, blog posts, newsletters, or author events. Respond to comments, participate in discussions, and show genuine interest in your readers' thoughts and feedback.
- Create an eye-catching book cover design. Invest in a professionally designed book cover that aligns with your genre and captivates potential readers. A visually appealing cover can make a significant impact on attracting readers and enhancing your overall brand image.
- Cultivate a consistent author voice. Develop a distinctive writing voice that reflects your brand and resonates with your target audience. Consistency in your writing style helps establish a recognizable brand identity and builds reader loyalty.
- Collaborate with influencers or fellow authors. Partnering with influencers or collaborating with fellow authors can expand your reach and introduce your brand to new audiences. Look for opportunities to cross-promote, participate in joint projects, or engage in guest blogging.
- Leverage reviews and testimonials. Positive reviews and testimonials can strengthen your brand's reputation and credibility. Encourage readers to leave reviews, share testimonials on your website or social media, and showcase positive feedback to build trust with potential readers.
- Stay true to your brand. As you grow and evolve as an author, continue to align your actions and writing projects with your brand identity. Consistency and authenticity will solidify your brand and help you build a loyal following.

THE ONE & ONLY UNCLE ME'SHORN

I AM NOT YOUR BLACK, AMERICA

Me'Shorn T Floyd Daniels

Trient Press®

UNLEASHING YOUR CREATIVE POTENTIAL:

Innovative Marketing Strategies for Authors

In today's digital era, authors find themselves navigating a dynamic landscape where technology presents both challenges and opportunities in promoting their work and connecting with readers. The vast reach of the internet and the power of technology have revolutionized the way authors can engage with their audience, making strategic marketing techniques more essential than ever before. In this article, we will delve into the key strategies that can empower authors to thrive in the digital realm, expand their reach to a wider audience, and unlock their full potential for success.

Embracing the Digital Transformation:

The advent of digital platforms and e-books has transformed the publishing industry, allowing authors to distribute their work to a global audience with unprecedented ease. By embracing this digital transformation, authors can capitalize on the convenience and accessibility of digital publishing, enabling them to reach readers across borders and time zones. This shift in approach opens up new possibilities and demands a strategic marketing mindset.

NEWS PROVIDED BY: Trient Press

Building an Author Platform:

ESTABLISHING A STRONG AUTHOR PLATFORM IS CRUCIAL FOR GAINING VISIBILITY AND CREDIBILITY. THIS INVOLVES CREATING A PROFESSIONAL WEBSITE, MAINTAINING ACTIVE SOCIAL MEDIA PROFILES, AND ENGAGING WITH READERS THROUGH CONSISTENT AND MEANINGFUL CONTENT.

BY CURATING AN ONLINE PRESENCE THAT REFLECTS YOUR UNIQUE BRAND AND EXPERTISE, YOU CAN ATTRACT AND RETAIN A DEDICATED FAN BASE.

Content Marketing:

Creating valuable content is a powerful way to attract and engage readers. Beyond writing books, authors can leverage various content formats such as blogs, articles, podcasts, and videos to provide insights, share expertise, and connect with their target audience. By consistently delivering high-quality content that resonates with readers, authors can establish themselves as thought leaders and foster a loyal following.

Harnessing the Power of Social Media:

Social media platforms have become indispensable tools for authors to connect directly with readers, build relationships, and generate buzz around their work. From sharing book updates to behind-the-scenes glimpses into the writing process, authors can leverage platforms like Instagram, Twitter, and Facebook to engage with their audience, host giveaways, and collaborate with influencers or fellow authors to expand their reach.

Influencer Marketing:

Partnering with influencers and industry experts can provide authors with valuable exposure and credibility. By collaborating with influencers who have a strong following and align with their genre or target audience, authors can tap into existing communities and gain access to new readers. Whether through book reviews, interviews, or joint promotional efforts, influencer marketing can significantly amplify an author's reach and boost book sales.

In the digital age, strategic marketing techniques are vital for authors to cut through the noise and connect with readers on a meaningful level. By building a strong author platform, creating valuable content, leveraging social media, collaborating with influencers, and harnessing the power of email marketing, authors can maximize their reach, amplify their brand, and achieve long-term success. Embracing these strategies in the ever-evolving digital landscape can position authors for growth and recognition in the highly competitive publishing industry.

Note: Please keep in mind that Forbes has its own editorial guidelines and standards. The above article is a general suggestion and may need to be tailored to meet their specific requirements and style.

MeShorn Daniels: Uncovering the Roots of Identity and Healing America

In the bustling city of Louisville, Kentucky, resides MeShorn Daniels, a man with a remarkable journey that spans from Miami to serving in the military and eventually finding his true calling as a writer. His story is one of resilience, self-discovery, and a deep desire to promote unity and healing in America.

Retiring from the military after twenty-one years of service, MeShorn Daniels settled in Louisville, where he has been a part of the community for over thirty years. His journey began as a cook, but little did he know that life had much more in store for him.

In a candid conversation with M.L. Ruscscak, MeShorn revealed that writing was not something he had ever considered. Having never attended formal classes or been a part of academic circles, he initially felt distant from the idea of becoming a writer. However, life had other plans for him.

It was during the COVID-19 pandemic that MeShorn came across a book by Dr. Nois Shelton, titled "America's Little Black Book." This eye-opening read sparked a profound realization in MeShorn. He began to question the labels of race and identity that society had placed upon him and others. The journey of introspection and self-discovery had begun.

In his book, "I'm Not your Black America," MeShorn delves into the historical roots of slavery in the United States and the impact it had on shaping identities. He challenges the commonly used terms "black" and "African American" and proposes the term "American Descendants of Slaves" as a more accurate reflection of his heritage. MeShorn believes that moving away from color-based labels can foster unity and understanding among all Americans.

As an author, MeShorn sees himself as a bearer of knowledge, aiming to help people unlearn and relearn their history. He advocates for embracing one's true identity and appreciating the diverse cultural heritage that makes America unique. His book serves as a powerful testament to the need for healing and reconciliation in the country.

The conversation with M.L. Ruscscak sheds light on the untold history of America's evolution, the exploitation of various immigrant groups, and the industrialization of slavery. MeShorn emphasizes that confronting the past and understanding its origins is essential to address the current issues of racism and division that persist in society.

"DON'T ALLOW YOURSELF TO BE CONSUMED BY THE ENVIRONMENT THAT YOU'RE BORN INTO. IT TAKES US LOVING OURSELF TO OVERCOME IT. YOU HAVE LEARN TO UNLEARN AND RELEARN WHO YOU ARE!"

MeShorn Daniels firmly believes that each human life holds infinite value, irrespective of color or background. He founded "God's Matter," a platform that advocates for unity and mutual respect among all citizens. He envisions a future where individuals from diverse backgrounds can come together in brotherhood, just as Martin Luther King Jr. once envisioned.

Through his book and advocacy work, MeShorn Daniels has become a beacon of hope and a voice of reason in America's pursuit of healing. As we look towards the future, his message serves as a call for all citizens to work together to build a more united and inclusive nation. The journey may be challenging, but with each step towards understanding and empathy, America can rewrite its history, embracing the diversity that lies at its core.

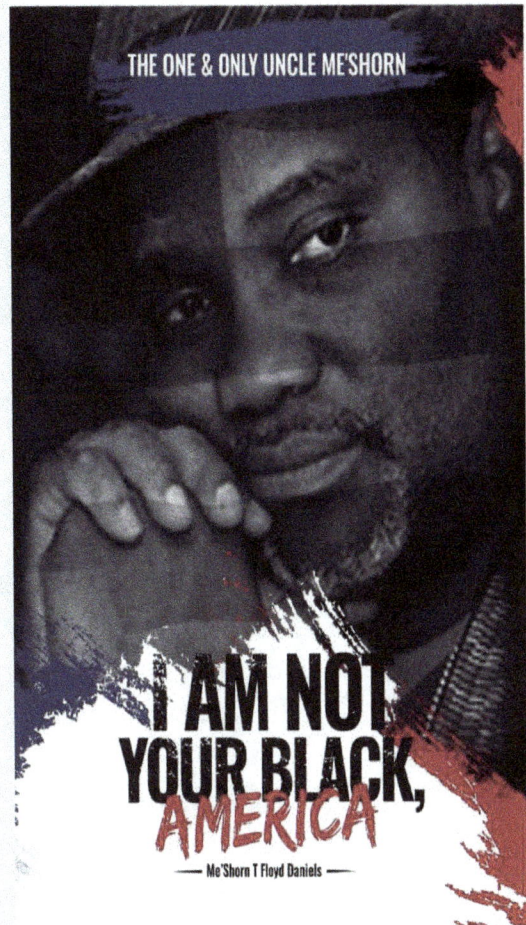

THE ONE & ONLY UNCLE ME'SHORN

I AM NOT YOUR BLACK, AMERICA

— Me'Shorn T Floyd Daniels —

"MeShorn's Book is going to challenge you. Y'all got to read that. I don't care if you like him or not. Doesn't matter! You gotta hear him. You gotta read him and try to understand him. This is a very important voice. And he's not a fringe voice within the black community." -Corbin Seavers Show

Find out more about Meshorn at:
www.trientpress.com
https://www.unclemeshorn.com/

Celebrating the Power of Positivity: An Interview with Kay Oliver

As the summer sun embraced the city, People Magazine had the pleasure of sitting down with the remarkable author, Kay Oliver. With five books already published and a sixth on the horizon, her talent for weaving captivating stories has not gone unnoticed. But what truly sets Kay apart is her commitment to spreading positivity and highlighting the unsung heroes of our world.

The conversation began with Kay reminiscing about her early writing days, tracing back to her sixth-grade speech contest. Little did she know that this first brush with writing would pave the way for a lifelong love affair with storytelling. "I've always loved writing," she said, "and after starting in the speech club, I went on to work in Hollywood. So I've been writing my whole life."

Reflecting on her journey, she shared a pivotal moment that inspired her to become an author. "My first experience in the speech contest was semi-discouraging," Kay recounted. "The judges thought my speech was so good that they believed my parents wrote it for me. It was a mix of both good and bad feelings at the time."

From that early encounter, Kay's passion for writing only intensified. Her very first published book, "Keeping Your Soul Intact in the Workplace," was based on her master's thesis. However, it was her fascination with archaeology and the ethical questions surrounding tomb excavation that birthed her first fiction book, "Disturbed Tombs."

"I've always been into archaeology," Kay explained. "I questioned the relentless digging up of every Egyptian tomb we find, while our own graveyards are considered sacred. That's what sparked the idea for 'Disturbed Tombs'— a fictional story centered around this very concept."

www.kayaoliver.com

As the interview progressed, Kay elaborated on her latest novel, "A Road to Alicia," which was inspired by a heartwarming news story she came across. "I saw a little story about a boy asking a man to teach him how to throw a leaf of baseball, and the man immediately said yes," she recalled. "That one instant decision to help and the boy's courage to ask for help inspired me to write the book."

In an era inundated with negative news, Kay's mission is to inject positivity back into the universe through her novels. "We rarely hear positive stories in the media," she lamented. "My books celebrate the simple acts of kindness that can change lives and ripple through communities."

When asked about her upcoming book, Kay revealed that it involved five schoolteachers in the Old West with a hidden secret. Drawing on her love for history, she poured herself into extensive research to ensure historical accuracy while infusing her signature positive touch.

Throughout the conversation, it was evident that Kay's characters were a driving force behind her stories. "I write strong, intelligent characters who respect and support one another," she beamed. "My readers often find themselves connecting with the characters, feeling like they could step into their shoes."

As our time together drew to a close, Kay expressed her joy at being recognized as one of the influential women in her city due to her writing. With her sixth book on the horizon and her dedication to the power of positivity, Kay Oliver is undoubtedly an author worth celebrating.

In a world hungry for inspiration and hope, Kay Oliver's novels provide a refreshing oasis of positivity. We eagerly await her upcoming works and the stories they will reveal. Keep an eye out for her latest book, as it promises to be another masterpiece born from her passion for history and storytelling.

ENTREPRENEUR TIPS AND TRICKS

Unlocking the Power of AI Broad Strokes for Successful Integration in Any Business

- Identify areas for AI integration: Begin by identifying specific areas within your business operations where AI can bring value. This could include tasks such as data analysis, customer support, inventory management, or predictive analytics. Look for repetitive or time-consuming tasks that could benefit from automation or enhanced decision-making capabilities.

- Educate yourself and your team: Familiarize yourself and your team with the basics of AI and its potential applications in your industry. Understanding the capabilities and limitations of AI will help you identify the most suitable use cases for implementation.

- Start small and scale up: Consider starting with small AI projects or pilot programs to test the feasibility and effectiveness of AI integration within your business. By starting small, you can minimize risks, gather valuable insights, and gradually expand AI implementation as you gain confidence and experience.

- Leverage AI-powered analytics: Take advantage of AI-powered analytics tools to gain deeper insights from your data. AI algorithms can analyze large volumes of data faster and more accurately than humans, helping you uncover patterns, trends, and actionable insights to inform your decision-making process.

- Enhance customer experience with AI: Explore AI-driven solutions to enhance your customer experience. Chatbots, virtual assistants, and AI-powered recommendation engines can improve customer interactions, provide personalized recommendations, and deliver faster and more efficient customer support.

- Automate repetitive tasks: Identify repetitive tasks in your business workflows that can be automated using AI. This could include data entry, report generation, email sorting, or social media scheduling. Automating these tasks frees up time for your team to focus on higher-value activities.

- Implement AI in marketing and sales: Utilize AI to optimize your marketing and sales efforts. AI-powered algorithms can help analyze customer behavior, segment audiences, personalize marketing campaigns, and automate lead scoring and nurturing processes.

- Prioritize data security and privacy: As you incorporate AI, ensure that you have robust security measures in place to protect sensitive data. Comply with relevant data protection regulations and establish clear policies for data handling and privacy.

- Foster a culture of AI adoption: Encourage a culture of learning and experimentation within your organization. Promote AI literacy among your employees and provide training opportunities to develop AI-related skills. Emphasize the value of AI as a tool for innovation and efficiency.

- Stay informed about AI advancements: AI is a rapidly evolving field, so it's important to stay informed about new developments, emerging technologies, and best practices. Follow industry publications, attend conferences or webinars, and engage in knowledge-sharing communities to stay updated on the latest AI trends and applications.

- Remember, integrating AI into your business requires careful planning, ongoing evaluation, and a willingness to adapt. By strategically incorporating AI technologies, you can unlock new efficiencies, enhance decision-making, and gain a competitive edge in your industry.

AI IN EVERYDAY USE: TRANSFORMING HOW WE LIVE AND INTERACT IN THE DIGITAL AGE

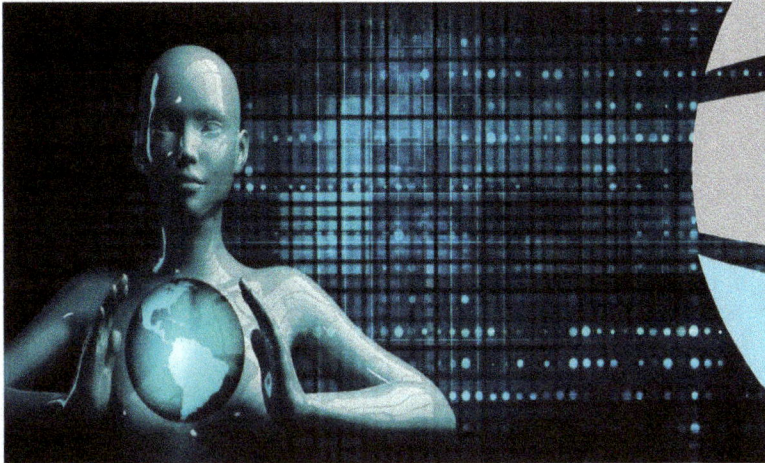

NEWS PROVIDED BY: TRIENT PRESS

In the rapidly evolving landscape of the digital age, artificial intelligence (AI) has emerged as a powerful force driving transformative change in our daily lives. From virtual assistants to personalized recommendations, AI technologies have seamlessly integrated into our routines, revolutionizing how we live, work, and interact. In this article, we will explore the incredible impact of AI in everyday use, showcasing its transformative potential and highlighting key areas where AI is reshaping our world.

AI has transformed the way we experience personalized content and services. Algorithms analyze vast amounts of data, tailoring recommendations based on our preferences and behavior. From streaming platforms suggesting shows we'll love to e-commerce sites presenting curated product selections, AI enhances our everyday interactions by catering to our individual needs and preferences.

1.0 Smart Homes and the Internet of Things (IoT):

The integration of AI and the Internet of Things (IoT) has made our homes smarter and more intuitive. AI-powered voice assistants, like Amazon's Alexa or Google Assistant, seamlessly control various connected devices, offering hands-free control over our environments. Whether adjusting the temperature, dimming the lights, or ordering groceries, AI-enabled smart homes have transformed mundane tasks into effortless experiences.

2. Virtual Assistants and Chatbots:

Virtual assistants and chatbots have become ubiquitous, providing instant support and enhancing productivity. These AI-driven companions, such as Apple's Siri or Microsoft's Cortana, help us with tasks like setting reminders, answering queries, and even managing our schedules. Chatbots, employed by businesses across industries, offer immediate customer service, resolving queries efficiently and enhancing user experiences.

3. AI in Healthcare:

The healthcare industry has witnessed remarkable advancements through AI. From disease diagnosis to personalized treatment plans, AI algorithms analyze vast medical data, assisting healthcare professionals in making informed decisions. AI also enables remote patient monitoring, predictive analytics for disease prevention, and precision medicine, leading to improved patient outcomes and optimized healthcare delivery.

4. AI for Enhanced Cybersecurity:

In an increasingly digitized world, AI plays a critical role in strengthening cybersecurity measures. AI algorithms detect and respond to cyber threats in real-time, bolstering defense systems against malware, phishing attacks, and data breaches. By continuously learning and adapting to evolving threats, AI-driven cybersecurity solutions provide proactive protection for individuals and organizations.

5. AI for Enhanced Cybersecurity:

In an increasingly digitized world, AI plays a critical role in strengthening cybersecurity measures. AI algorithms detect and respond to cyber threats in real-time, bolstering defense systems against malware, phishing attacks, and data breaches. By continuously learning and adapting to evolving threats, AI-driven cybersecurity solutions provide proactive protection for individuals and organizations.

New Releases

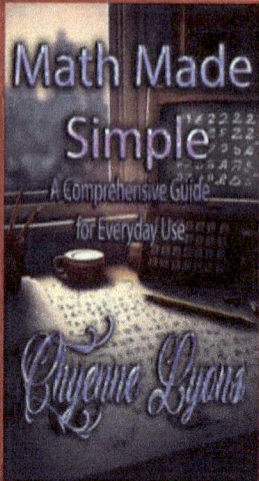

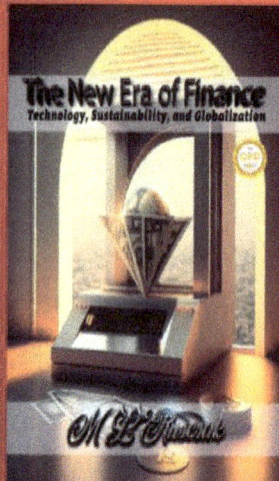

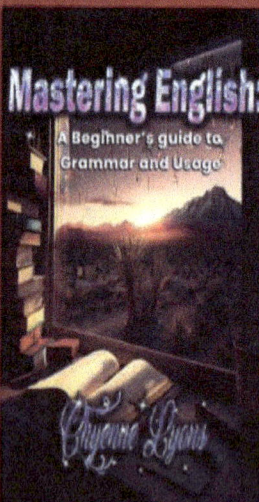

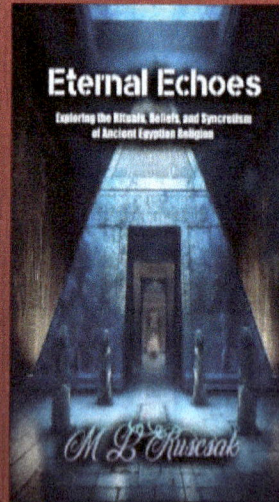

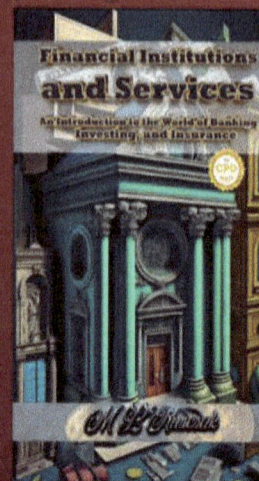

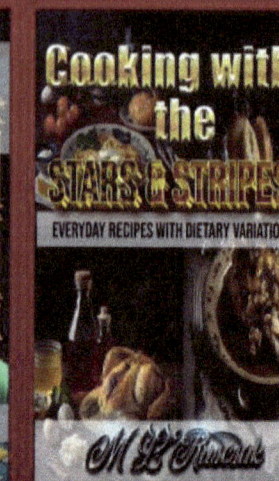

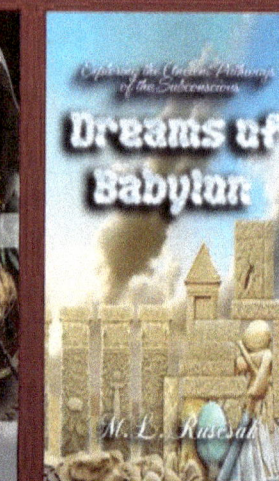

EMBRACE, DON'T FEAR:
Overcoming AI's Impact
ON JOBS AND USHERING IN A NEW ERA OF OPPORTUNITY

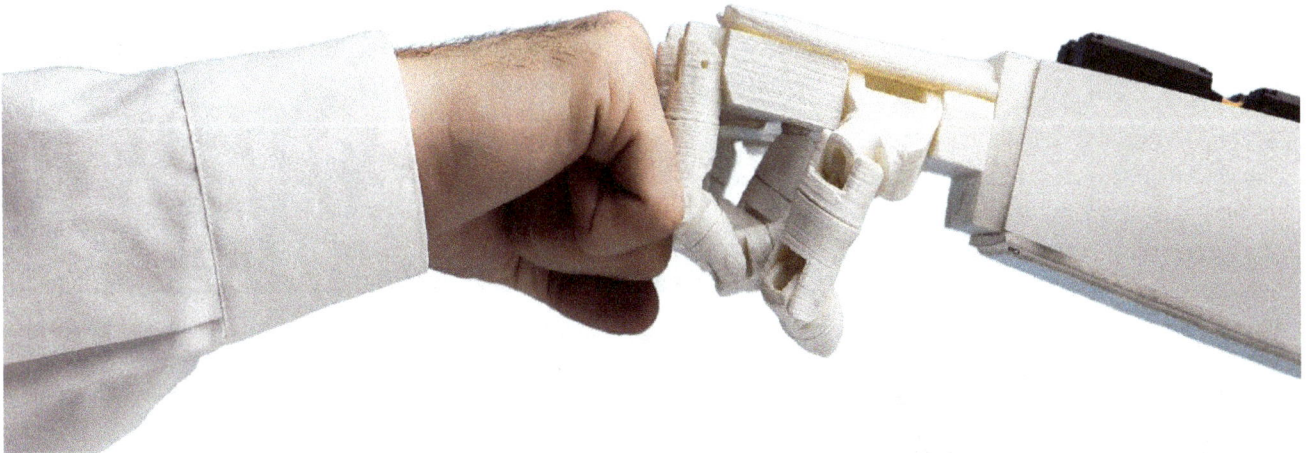

Business

In the ever-evolving landscape of the business world, the rise of artificial intelligence (AI) has sparked both excitement and apprehension. As AI technologies become more sophisticated, concerns about job displacement and workforce disruption have been amplified. However, this fear should not overshadow the vast potential for growth and new opportunities that AI brings. In this article, we will explore how adopting a positive business mindset can help professionals and organizations overcome the fear of AI coming for their jobs and instead embrace a future brimming with innovation, collaboration, and personal growth.

7

Understand the Evolution of Work:

Throughout history, technological advancements have led to shifts in the job market. AI is no exception. Rather than fear job displacement, embrace the idea that AI will redefine the nature of work. With repetitive and mundane tasks automated, professionals can focus on higher-value activities, leveraging their creativity, critical thinking, and emotional intelligence to drive business success.

Embrace Lifelong Learning:

To thrive in the AI-driven world, professionals must adopt a mindset of continuous learning. Upskilling and reskilling will be crucial to remain relevant and adaptable to changing job requirements. Companies that invest in employee training and development empower their workforce to embrace AI as a tool for personal and professional growth.

Collaborate with AI:

AI isn't here to take over our jobs but to team up with us. When we work together with AI technologies, we can boost productivity and make smarter decisions. Treat AI like a partner, tapping into its capabilities to enhance your skills, increase efficiency, and uncover valuable insights that drive your strategic decisions.

Foster an Innovative Culture:

Let's infuse our organization with an innovative spirit where everyone is encouraged to explore new ideas and embrace change. Empower teams to find areas where AI can streamline processes, improve products, and create fresh solutions for our customers. Embracing a growth mindset will fuel innovation and put us on the fast track to success.

Embrace Creativity and Problem-Solving:

AI might handle the routine stuff, but it can't match the unique creativity and problem-solving skills we humans have. Celebrate the value of human intelligence when tackling complex challenges. Let's nurture and develop these skills in our workforce and create an environment where AI and human ingenuity work hand in hand.

Reshape Roles, Not Say Goodbye:

Forget the idea that AI will steal jobs; it's here to redefine them! As some tasks get automated, new roles will emerge to manage AI systems analyze data, and implement AI-driven strategies. We'll be proactive in identifying these new opportunities and make sure our team is well-equipped to thrive in these roles.

Conclusion:

Overcoming the fear of AI taking our jobs means changing our perspective. Let's see AI as a catalyst for positive change and growth. By embracing a growth mindset, continuously learning, collaborating with AI, and nurturing an innovative culture, we'll embrace the boundless possibilities of the AI era. Let's harness AI's potential to boost productivity, improve decision-making, and unlock exciting new opportunities. With confidence, we'll embrace the future, knowing that partnering with AI will shape a world where human brilliance and technology combine to create a brighter, more prosperous future for all.

For more tips and ideas to become a successful business owner find us at www.trientpressmagazine.com.

Embracing the AI Revolution:

Efficiency and Innovation Unleashed

Welcome to the brave new world of AI in business, where the possibilities are as vast as the universe. Just imagine having a powerful ally by your side, capable of transforming your business in ways you never thought possible. If you're curious about how AI can supercharge your efficiency and ignite innovation, well, you're in for a treat!

AI isn't just another fancy buzzword; it's a game-changer that has the potential to revolutionize the way you do business. Prepare yourself to embark on an exciting journey where technology meets creativity, and the results are nothing short of extraordinary.

Remember those tedious, time-consuming tasks that used to weigh you down? Say goodbye to them! With AI as your trusty sidekick, you can bid farewell to hours spent on repetitive chores. Instead, embrace the newfound freedom and productivity that AI brings to your everyday life.

As a business owner or entrepreneur, you understand that time is one of your most precious resources. AI understands it too! By streamlining workflows and automating mundane processes, AI gives you the gift of time – time to focus on what truly matters: crafting innovative strategies, fostering creativity, and connecting with your customers on a deeper level.

Melisa Ruscsak
Editor-in-Chief

Trient Press Magazine

AUGUST / SEPTEMBER 2023

Speaking of customers, they're the heartbeat of your business, and AI knows how to speak their language. Dive into a world where AI analyzes mountains of data to reveal invaluable insights into customer preferences and behavior patterns. Armed with this knowledge, you can craft personalized experiences that resonate with your audience, building strong and lasting relationships that drive loyalty and advocacy.

Embrace the power of AI as a game-changer!

But that's not all. AI isn't just about making your life easier; it's a gateway to innovation. As AI unlocks the secrets hidden within your data, you'll gain a fresh perspective on your business. Identify untapped opportunities, spot emerging trends, and make informed decisions that position your business at the forefront of your industry.

Embrace the thrill of the unknown as you venture into this uncharted territory. Embrace the power of AI to enhance your efficiency, streamline your operations, and empower your team to reach new heights of success. This isn't just a journey of technological advancement; it's a journey of self-discovery, where you uncover the true potential of your business and unlock opportunities that were once beyond your imagination.

So, get ready to be amazed, get ready to be inspired, and get ready to harness the full potential of AI in your business. The future is bright, and the possibilities are limitless. With AI as your trusted partner, you're equipped to conquer new horizons and make your mark in this brave new world of business. Welcome aboard!

Say Goodbye to Mundane Tasks:

Say goodbye to mundane tasks and embrace a newfound sense of freedom and productivity! Picture this: you wake up, and instead of being swamped by an overwhelming sea of repetitive tasks, you feel empowered and ready to tackle the day head-on. Thanks to AI, that dream becomes a delightful reality!

Gone are the days of drowning in paperwork or spending endless hours on mind-numbing data entry. AI swoops in as your trusty sidekick, taking care of those tedious chores with lightning speed and unparalleled accuracy. With AI by your side, you and your team can bid farewell to the mundane and say hello to efficiency like never before.

> By taking action, you are one step closer to the life you always desire!

Imagine the possibilities when you're no longer bogged down by repetitive tasks. You'll have the time and mental space to focus on the big picture – the innovative ideas that drive your business forward, the creative strategies that set you apart from the competition, and the personal connections that strengthen your customer relationships.

AI is the ultimate efficiency booster, and it doesn't discriminate. Whether you're a solopreneur or leading a team, AI empowers everyone to reclaim their time and channel it towards what truly matters. Think about how much more you can accomplish when you're not buried under a mountain of paperwork or chained to data entry tasks.

With mundane tasks out of the way, you'll experience a newfound sense of freedom and inspiration. As AI handles the repetitive, you can focus on the meaningful – the high-impact tasks that align with your vision and goals. Use your time to brainstorm, strategize, and explore innovative solutions that propel your business to new heights.

AI's efficiency isn't just a nice-to-have; it's a game-changer that elevates your business to a whole new level. Empower your team to unleash their creativity and problem-solving skills, knowing that AI has their back on the administrative front. As AI streamlines your workflows, you'll witness an uplift in team morale and productivity.

So, say farewell to the mundane, and let AI be the catalyst for a more efficient and inspired business journey. Embrace the gift of time, made possible by AI's unparalleled capabilities. Get ready to transform your workdays from monotonous to meaningful, and watch your business soar to new heights of success!

In this brave new world of AI, mundane tasks are a thing of the past, replaced by a newfound sense of freedom and productivity. With AI as your trusty sidekick, you wake up ready to conquer the day, unburdened by overwhelming chores. . Embrace the power of AI as the ultimate efficiency booster, catering to businesses of all sizes and empowering everyone to reclaim their time for more impactful pursuits.

epreneur

for Authors & Entrepreneurs

$10.99

Trientrepreneur

ent Press Publication for Authors & Entrepreneurs $10.99

ue 4 | July 2021

ATURED
er Special Agent,
Author Link

ARTICLES
ur Time Management
Tactics for Busy
entrepreneurs

ism Can Help
nd Strengthen
the Mind

TIPS
Must have information
for both authors and
entrepreneurs

entrepreneur

blication for Authors & Entrepreneurs

$10.99

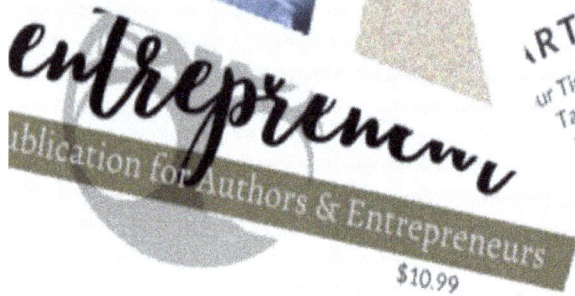

TRIENTREPRENEUR
MAGAZINE
WHAT'S IN YOUR TOOL BOX

Spotlight on a Successful Business
TechGrowth Solutions

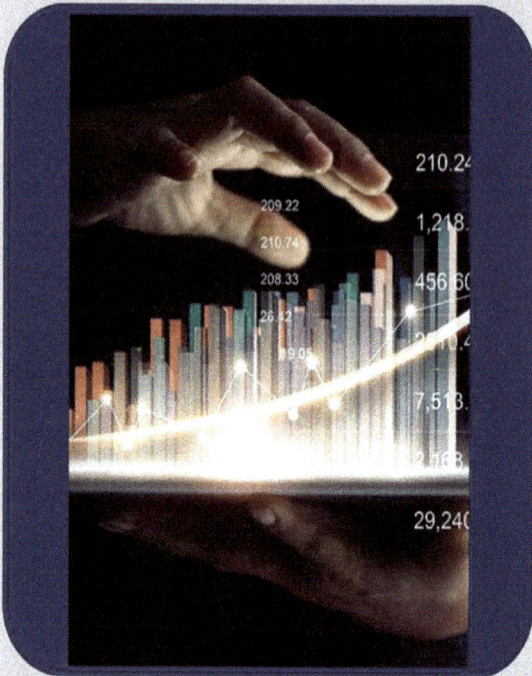

Let me tell you the inspiring story of TechGrowth Solutions, a small but mighty software development company that's making waves in the business world with the help of AI.

Once upon a time, TechGrowth Solutions started humbly, serving local businesses with their tailor-made software solutions. They were driven by passion and determination, but as their reputation grew, so did the demand for their services. Suddenly, they found themselves juggling multiple projects, and the pressure was on to maintain top-notch quality while keeping up with the increasing workload.

That's when they decided to harness the power of AI to level up their game. They adopted AI-powered project management tools that automated the repetitive tasks and made resource allocation a breeze. Suddenly, they had more time and energy to focus on delivering exceptional results to their clients.

But it didn't stop there. TechGrowth Solutions had their eyes on the bigger picture, and they knew AI could unlock untapped potential for their business. With AI-driven analytics at their fingertips, they delved deep into customer preferences and market trends. Armed with these invaluable insights, they crafted personalized solutions that hit the bullseye with their target audience.

And guess what? Their clients loved it! The word of mouth spread like wildfire, and their client base expanded beyond their wildest dreams. International clients started knocking on their virtual door, seeking their top-notch services from across the globe.

This game-changing move not only skyrocketed their revenue but also allowed them to explore new markets and untapped opportunities. Their journey with AI has been nothing short of a transformation, taking them from a local player to a global contender.

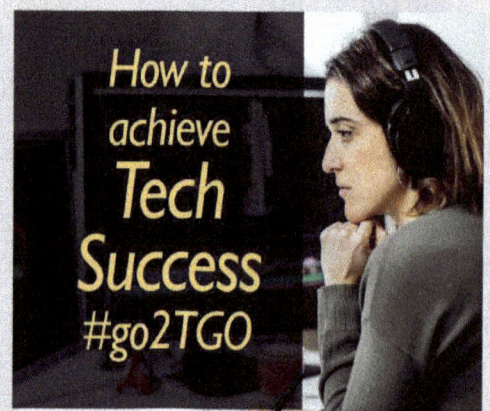

How to achieve **Tech Success** #go2TGO

TechGrowth Solutions' story is a testament to the game-changing potential of AI for small businesses. They've embraced innovation with open arms, and it's paid off in ways they could have never imagined. So, if you're a small business owner looking to scale and thrive, take a page out of TechGrowth Solutions' playbook and let AI be your business ally. The future is bright, and the possibilities are limitless!

New Release

By: M.L. Ruscsak

Exploring the Ancient Pathways
of the Subconscious

Dreams of
Babylon

M.L. Ruscsak

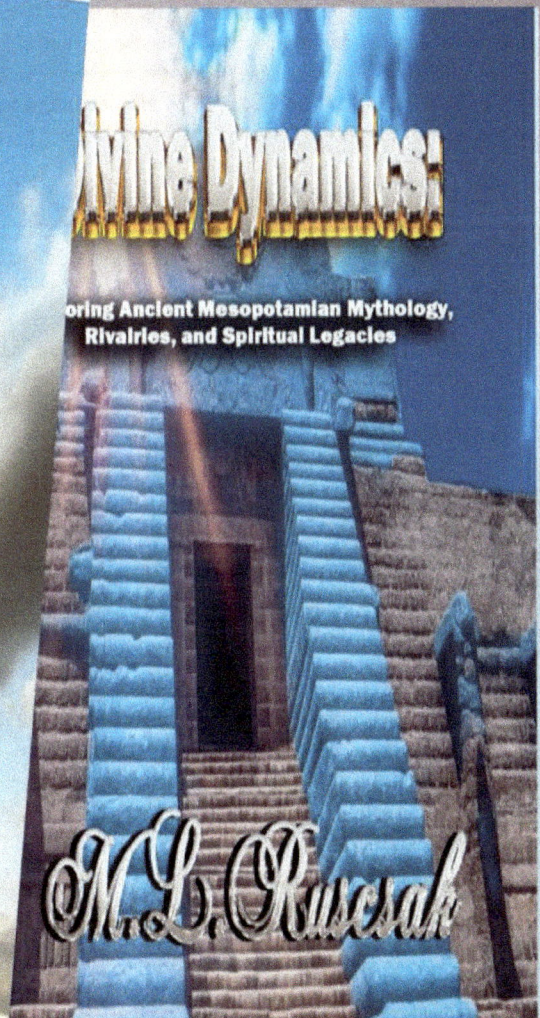

Divine Dynamics:

...oring Ancient Mesopotamian Mythology,
Rivalries, and Spiritual Legacies

M.L. Ruscsak

Trient Press.

CASE STUDY: A COMPANY'S JOURNEY FROM TURBULENCE TO SUCCESS

Apple

Apple Inc., a company that needs no introduction, has left an indelible mark on the tech industry and the world at large. Founded in 1976 by Steve Jobs, Steve Wozniak, and Ronald Wayne in a humble garage, the company's early days were marked by the passion and determination of its young founders. Little did they know that their journey would be a rollercoaster of ups and downs, failures and triumphs, making Apple's history an awe-inspiring tale of perseverance, reinvention, and visionary leadership.

In its infancy, Apple's first product, the Apple I computer, was a daring leap into the uncharted territory of personal computing. However, despite its groundbreaking design and potential, initial sales were modest, and the road to success was fraught with obstacles. But this didn't deter the tenacious founders. Undeterred by early setbacks, they forged ahead, refining their vision and pushing the boundaries of innovation.

The early '80s brought both success and turbulence for Apple. The company's iconic Macintosh computer captured the imagination of the public with its groundbreaking graphical user interface. Yet, internal power struggles and strategic missteps led to Steve Jobs' departure from Apple in 1985, leaving the company in a state of uncertainty.

However, as the saying goes, "What doesn't kill you makes you stronger." And that was precisely the case for Apple. During Jobs' absence, Apple faced immense challenges, struggling to compete against the dominance of Microsoft and the ever-growing PC market. But the seeds of reinvention were sown during this period.

In 1997, to the astonishment of the tech world, Steve Jobs returned to Apple, bringing with him a renewed sense of purpose and a laser-sharp focus on innovation. Under Jobs' visionary leadership, Apple initiated a transformative journey that would redefine the company and the entire tech landscape.

The iMac, introduced in 1998, was a statement of Apple's commitment to groundbreaking design and ease of use. Its vibrant colors and distinctive form factor captured the imagination of consumers, breathing new life into Apple's product lineup and paving the way for the company's resurgence.

But Apple was just getting started. The early 2000s saw the introduction of two game-changing products: the iPod and the iTunes Store. The iPod revolutionized how people consumed music, while the iTunes Store provided a seamless platform for legal music downloads, changing the music industry forever.

Then, in 2007, Apple unleashed its game-changer: the iPhone. The iconic device combined a phone, music player, and internet communicator into one sleek package, setting a new standard for smartphones and kickstarting the mobile revolution. The App Store, launched in conjunction with the iPhone, created a thriving ecosystem of apps that further solidified Apple's position as a tech trailblazer.

The innovations didn't stop there. In 2010, Apple introduced the iPad, a tablet device that redefined how we interacted with technology. Its intuitive touch interface and extensive app ecosystem created a new product category, disrupting traditional computing and shaping the future of mobile computing.

Throughout its journey, Apple's success can be attributed to its unwavering commitment to innovation, its emphasis on user experience, and its relentless pursuit of excellence. The company's ability to reinvent itself, staying ahead of the curve, has allowed it to thrive in an ever-evolving industry.

From humble beginnings in a garage to becoming one of the most valuable companies in the world.

Apple's trajectory serves as a beacon of inspiration for entrepreneurs and dreamers alike. Its legacy of visionary leadership, resilience, and the relentless pursuit of greatness will continue to shape the tech industry for generations to come. In a world where innovation reigns supreme, Apple stands tall as a testament to what can be achieved through determination, passion, and the unwavering belief in the power of imagination.

The Early Struggles & The Departure of Steve Jobs

In the late 1970s, the ambitious trio of Steve Jobs, Steve Wozniak, and Ronald Wayne unveiled their audacious creation - the Apple I computer, a groundbreaking device that would ignite the flames of the personal computing revolution. The Apple I was a marvel of innovation, boasting a user-friendly design and remarkable potential, but its path to success was not without hurdles.

One of the significant challenges Apple faced during this early phase was the limited distribution of the Apple I. Operating out of the founders' garage, the company struggled to reach a broader audience, hindering the widespread adoption of their revolutionary product. Additionally, the Apple I's relatively high price point compared to competitors posed another obstacle, making it a less accessible option for potential customers in a market dominated by more affordable alternatives.

Despite these challenges, Apple's co-founders persevered, refining their vision and learning from their initial setbacks. The Apple I, though not a commercial success in its own right, laid the foundation for Apple's future innovations and set the stage for the brand's enduring legacy.

In the mid-1980s, Apple experienced rapid growth, driven by its innovative product lineup and increasing popularity among tech enthusiasts. However, this very success brought internal tensions to the forefront, and a power struggle ensued within the company's leadership. Tragically, the visionary co-founder Steve Jobs found himself at odds with the board of directors and was eventually forced out of the company he had helped create.

Jobs' departure marked a tumultuous period for Apple, and the company faced numerous challenges in his absence. Without his influential leadership, Apple's product lineup struggled to compete with the rising dominance of Microsoft and other PC manufacturers. Internal uncertainty and lack of a clear direction left the company in a vulnerable position.

Nevertheless, true to Apple's spirit of innovation, adversity became a catalyst for change. The departure of Steve Jobs forced the company to reevaluate its approach, leading to a period of introspection and a quest for reinvention.

Little did the world know that this departure would prove temporary, and Jobs would later return to Apple, ready to lead the company into an era of unparalleled success. But that was yet to come. For now, Apple's journey had been defined by ups and downs, an inspiring tale of resilience and the determination to change the world through technology.

The Return of Steve Jobs and Product Reinvention:

In the late 1990s, Apple found itself at a critical crossroads. The once trailblazing company was grappling with declining market share and financial losses, and its future seemed uncertain. However, a glimmer of hope emerged when, in 1997, the prodigal visionary, Steve Jobs, returned to Apple as CEO. His second coming would prove to be a turning point in the company's history, marking the beginning of an extraordinary transformation.

Under Jobs' visionary leadership, Apple initiated a series of bold and strategic moves that would reshape the company and the tech industry forever. Embracing the ethos of innovation and user-centric design, Apple set out on a mission to redefine the consumer electronics landscape.

In 1998, Apple unleashed the iMac, an all-in-one computer that shattered traditional notions of how computers should look and feel. The colorful, user-friendly iMac was a breath of fresh air, capturing the imagination of consumers and signaling a new era for Apple. Its resounding success marked the start of the company's resurgence and ignited a spark of confidence within the organization.

1976   1977   1995   1998   2001   2007   2015

Logo History: Evolution of the Apple Logo

Then, in 2007, Apple unleashed its game-changing masterpiece: the iPhone.

This revolutionary device seamlessly combined a phone, music player, and internet communicator into one elegantly designed package. The iPhone's intuitive touch interface, coupled with the App Store ecosystem, revolutionized the smartphone industry, forever changing the way people interacted with technology. Apple had not just created a device; it had created a cultural phenomenon.

Building on its success, Apple continued to push boundaries. In 2010, the company introduced the iPad, a groundbreaking tablet that reimagined how we consumed media and interacted with technology. The iPad's stunning display and intuitive interface carved out a new product category, sparking a tablet revolution that transcended industries and applications.

Through these strategic moves, Apple solidified its position as a technology leader, setting itself apart from competitors and capturing the hearts of consumers worldwide. The company's journey from failure to success is a testament to the power of resilience, innovation, and visionary leadership.

Today, Apple's impact on the world is undeniable. Its products and services have become integral parts of modern life, shaping industries, and touching the lives of millions. The company's relentless pursuit of excellence and its commitment to pushing the boundaries of technology continue to inspire and revolutionize the world. As Apple continues to innovate and create, its story serves as a beacon of hope and a reminder that even in the face of adversity, greatness is within reach for those who dare to dream and have the courage to reinvent themselves.

In conclusion, Apple's extraordinary journey from failure to success is a remarkable testament to the enduring power of innovation, unwavering determination, and visionary leadership. Throughout its history, the company has exemplified the spirit of resilience, navigating through turbulent times and emerging stronger than ever before.

Central to Apple's triumph is its unwavering commitment to reinvention. When faced with challenges and setbacks, Apple didn't shy away from change; it embraced it wholeheartedly. From the early struggles of the Apple I to the internal turmoil during Steve Jobs' departure, the company never lost sight of its mission to create products that would resonate with consumers and enrich their lives.

Moreover, Apple's success is deeply rooted in its unwavering focus on the customer experience. Every product and service that bears the iconic Apple logo is meticulously designed with the user in mind. This relentless dedication to user-centric design has set Apple apart, creating a unique emotional connection with its customers that goes beyond mere technology.

By consistently delivering groundbreaking and innovative products, such as the iMac, iPod, iPhone, and iPad, Apple has not only transformed itself but also redefined entire industries. Each new release captures the world's attention, driving cultural shifts and setting new standards for excellence in technology.

Today, as one of the world's most valuable and influential companies, Apple remains at the forefront of technological advancement. Its unyielding commitment to pushing the boundaries of what is possible continues to inspire and shape the future of innovation.

From the charismatic leadership of Steve Jobs to the collective dedication of Apple's talented teams, the company's journey is an enduring example of how visionary leadership, coupled with a culture of innovation, can transform failure into resounding success.

As we look ahead, one thing is certain: Apple's journey is far from over. The company's insatiable thirst for innovation ensures that it will continue to surprise and captivate the world with products that have the power to change lives and leave a lasting impact on society.

In the ever-evolving world of technology, Apple's story stands as an emblem of what is possible when courage, creativity, and passion converge. As we embrace the brave new frontier of innovation, we can look to Apple as a guiding light, reminding us that, with the right blend of innovation and determination, we too can transcend limitations and reach heights we once thought impossible.

In the end, Apple's journey is not just about a company's rise from the ashes; it is a testament to the human spirit's indomitable will to dream, create, and shape the world we live in. With each new chapter, Apple continues to inspire the world and remind us all that innovation knows no bounds. The journey from failure to success is a testament to what can be achieved when we dare to think differently and believe in the power of our imagination.

M.L. Ruscsak

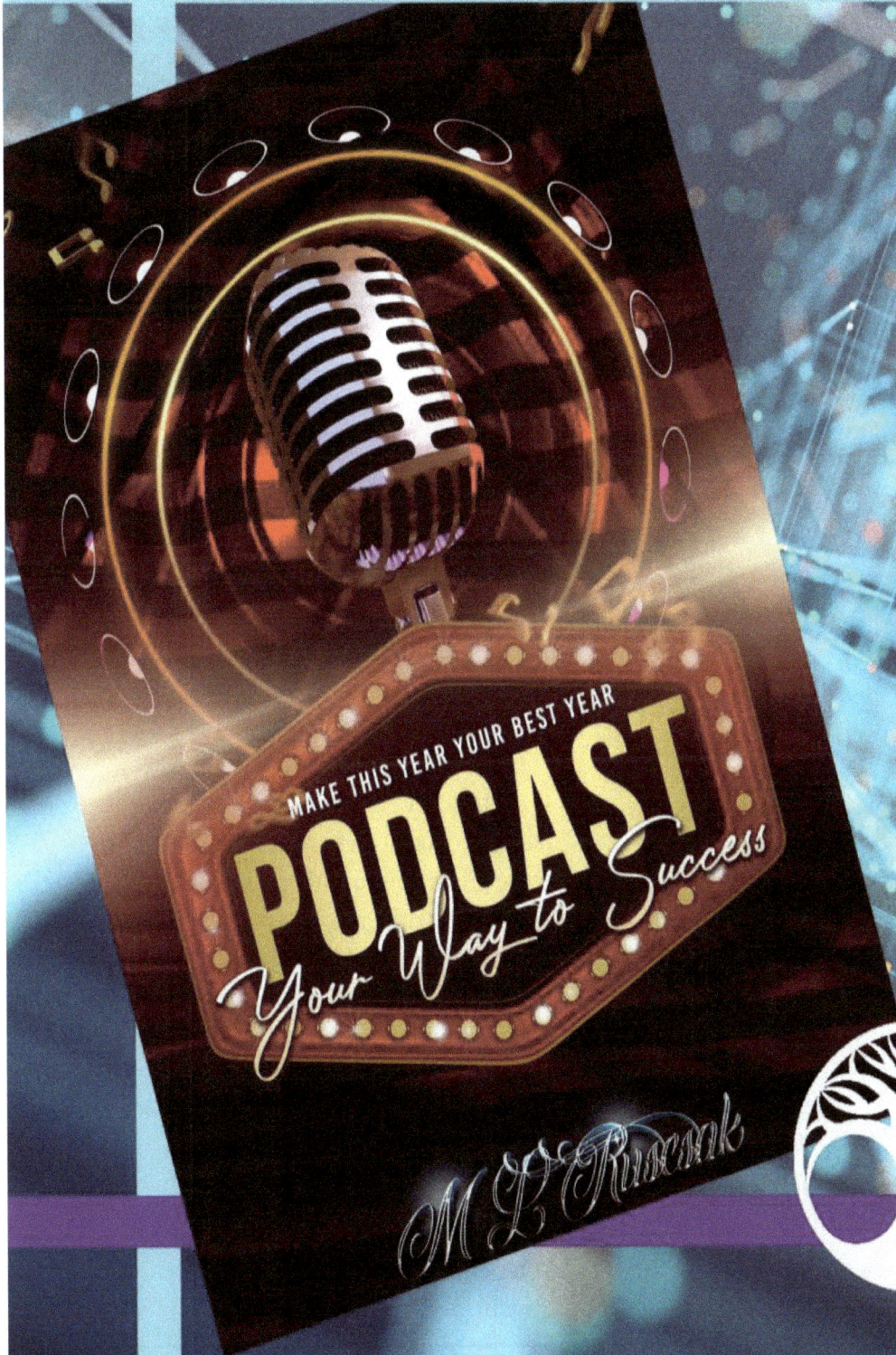

MAKE THIS YEAR YOUR BEST YEAR
PODCAST
Your Way to Success

M.L. Ruscsak

Trient Press

PRESS RELEASE

01 August, 2023

For Immediate Release

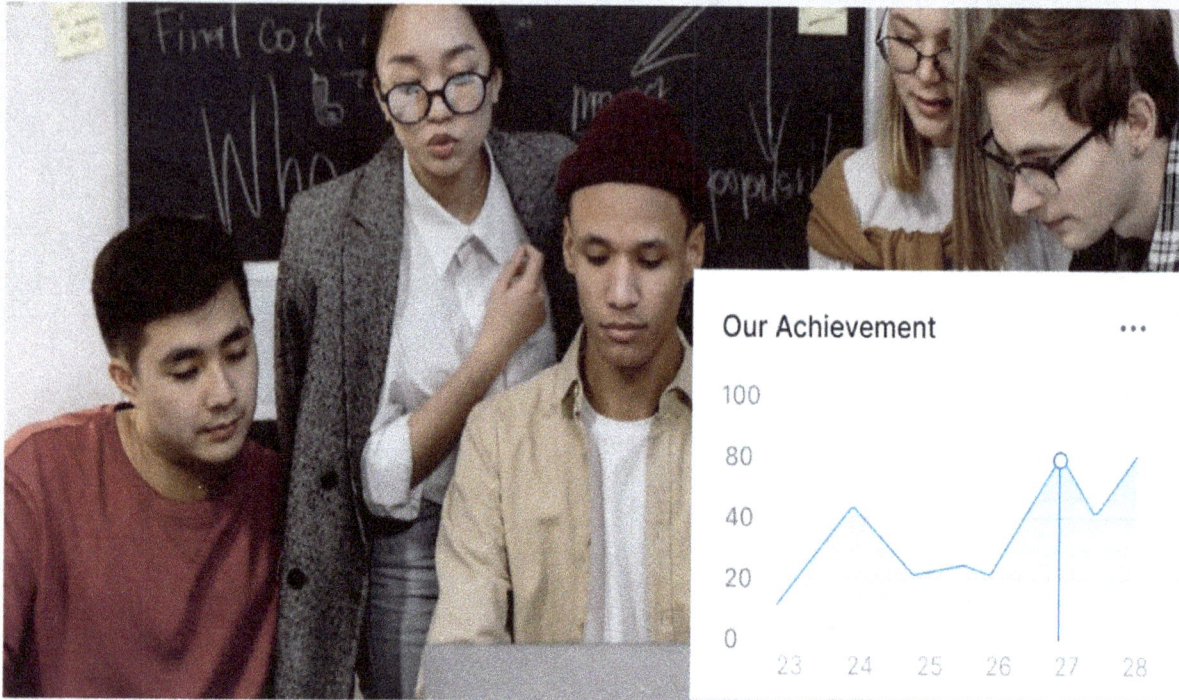

Our Achievement · · ·

AMPLIFY YOUR SUCCESS AND MAXIMIZE PROFITS WITH ATS LEADS

Imagine leveraging Google's vast public database, social media platforms, targeted hashtags, and precise email lists to connect with your prospective clients. Discover customers who are eager to buy from you. Tap into an abundant wealth of business opportunities with our precision targeting. Seize the moment, close lucrative deals, and watch your revenue skyrocket! 💼 💰

With us, you're not just unlocking leads. You're unlocking the path to exponential growth.

Navigating Changes in Your Industry
Ai4: Uniting the Global AI Ecosystem

Welcome to the extraordinary world of Ai4, the preeminent AI for business community that unites the global AI ecosystem through a dynamic blend of events, media, and resources. Our mission is to provide a common framework for industries as we step into an era of responsible human-machine collaboration. Through our premium conferences, we offer multi-day experiences brimming with innovation, top-notch speakers, and AI companies at the forefront of transformation. Don't miss our upcoming event at MGM Grand Las Vegas, Nevada, from Aug 7-10. Join our esteemed Leadership Council, where influential members help shape our events and ensure we deliver cutting-edge information essential for AI leaders' success.

Much like in crypto trading, setting a risk threshold is vital for businesses navigating the AI space. Determining the right amount of risk a company can accommodate and pattern their strategies accordingly lays the groundwork for responsible AI implementation. Building a secure trading ecosystem for your AI integration, just as you would for your crypto investments, is equally crucial. Ensuring privacy, security, and control over your AI systems protects your assets from potential vulnerabilities.

Researching and understanding the specific risks associated with different AI technologies, much like exploring the nuances of various crypto coins, helps businesses make informed decisions. Diversifying your investment portfolio in AI solutions ensures that you don't place all your hopes on one technology, mitigating potential risks and maximizing opportunities.

Finally, having an exit strategy for AI integration is just as prudent as planning for an exit strategy in crypto trading. Recognizing the circumstances that may require a shift in allegiance to a different AI solution or even stepping back from certain technologies ensures companies can adapt and thrive in a rapidly changing environment.

AS WE DIVE INTO THE EVER-EVOLVING LANDSCAPE OF AI, IT'S CRUCIAL TO ACKNOWLEDGE THE RISKS AND OPPORTUNITIES THAT COME WITH IT. JUST AS IN THE CRYPTO TRADING WORLD, WHERE RISK MANAGEMENT IS ESSENTIAL, BUSINESSES TOO MUST ADOPT A LEVELHEADED APPROACH WHEN EMBRACING AI TECHNOLOGY. FROM THE EARLY STRUGGLES OF APPLE INC. TO ITS REMARKABLE SUCCESS TODAY, WE SEE THE POWER OF INNOVATION AND DETERMINATION IN TRANSFORMING FAILURES INTO TRIUMPHS.

As we continue our AI journey, let's embrace the lessons from the crypto trading world and incorporate risk management into our AI strategies. The way we respond to challenges and opportunities will be pivotal in shaping our success in the AI-powered future. With Ai4 as your trusted partner, we're here to guide you through this transformational journey, harnessing the full potential of AI and building a future that seamlessly blends human ingenuity with the limitless possibilities of technology. Together, we'll unlock a brave new world of innovation, collaboration, and progress. Welcome aboard!

Ai4 2023

A Journey of Resilience and Empowerment: An Interview with Larry Thornton

M.L. Ruscsak

"Meet Larry Thornton: A Living Inspiration of Breaking Barriers and Building a Better Community"

Corporate Titles:

- CEO (Chief Executive Officer) of Coca-Cola.
- Chairman of the Audit Committee at Coca-Cola (served on the Board of Directors).
- Board Member of Sonova's Bank.

In a candid and inspiring interview, M.L. Ruscscak sits down with Larry Thornton, a remarkable individual whose life journey has been nothing short of transformative. From facing adversity during the tumultuous times of the 1960s in the American South to becoming a successful CEO and author, Larry Thornton's story is a testament to the power of resilience and the refusal to let past missteps define one's future.

M.L. Ruscscak: Welcome, Larry Thornton! It's truly an honor to have you here with us today.

Larry Thornton: Thank you, M.L. I'm excited to be here and share my story.

M.L. Ruscscak: Your journey began in the 1960s, a challenging time in our culture, especially in the South. Yet, you managed to break barriers and pave your way to success. What was it like for you during those years?

Larry Thornton: It was indeed a difficult time, but I believe that facing adversity can lead to incredible growth and opportunities. I was one of six students accepted to an all-white school, which drew significant media attention. That experience played a crucial role in shaping my outlook on life.

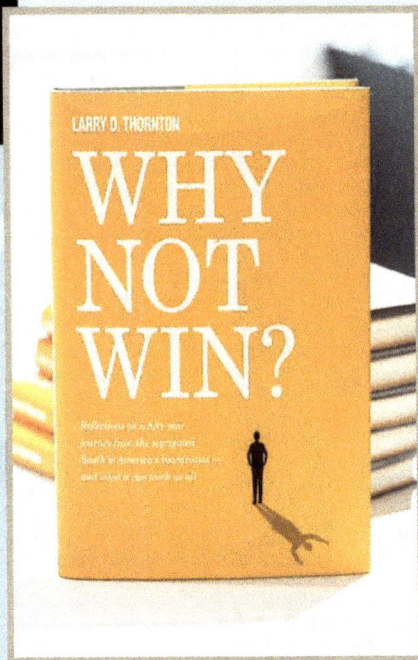

M.L. Ruscscak: And look at where you are now, a CEO of a corporation! It's amazing.

Larry Thornton: Thank you! It goes to show that we shouldn't let our past define us. By refusing to accept the societal messages of worthlessness, I was able to overcome challenges and achieve more than I ever thought possible.

M.L. Ruscscak: That's truly inspiring. Your story is a testament to the power of believing in oneself. Can you tell us about the turning point in your life, the moment you realized your worth?

Larry Thornton: The turning point for me was in high school when I had a teacher, Miss Nichols, who saw something in me that others didn't. She encouraged me to pursue my potential and made me realize that I was capable of so much more. Her belief in me changed the trajectory of my life.

M.L. Ruscscak: It's incredible how one person's belief and encouragement can make all the difference. You've mentioned the importance of working on oneself. Could you elaborate on that?

Larry Thornton: Absolutely. I believe that some of the most challenging work we can do is on ourselves. Changing our thinking, improving our attitudes, and developing personal disciplines are crucial for personal growth and success. When we work on ourselves, we become better equipped to contribute positively to our communities.

M.L. Ruscscak: That's a profound insight. It's essential to remember that building a better community starts with self-improvement. How do you plan to spread this message further?

Larry Thornton: I've established the "Why Not Win Institute" with the aim of reaching as many people as possible. We're using my book "Why Not Win?" and our newly released graphic novel to engage with younger audiences. By visiting college campuses and speaking to students, we hope to inspire the next generation to believe in themselves and work towards a better future.

M.L. Ruscscak: That's fantastic! Building a better community by empowering individuals is truly commendable. Larry, thank you for sharing your incredible journey with us today.

Larry Thornton: Thank you, M.L. It's been a pleasure, and I hope our conversation can inspire others to embrace their worth and strive for greatness.

In a world where obstacles can be discouraging, Larry Thornton's story is a beacon of hope and motivation. He exemplifies how resilience, self-belief, and a commitment to building a better community can lead to remarkable achievements. Let us all take inspiration from Larry's words and work towards making a positive impact on ourselves and the world around us. As Larry Thornton would say, "Why not win?" For the full interview tune in to Dove and Dragon Radio on all podcast stations.

The Power of Networking:

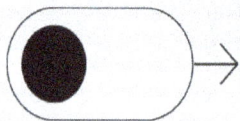

The Need for Lead Generation

In the vast and ever-evolving landscape of business, success is often determined by the strength of relationships and the ability to connect with others. Welcome to the world of networking - a strategic tool that opens doors, creates opportunities, and propels businesses to new heights of growth and success. In this digital age where connections are more critical than ever, networking has taken center stage as a powerhouse for lead generation. It goes beyond exchanging business cards or making small talk at events; networking is about building genuine connections, listening attentively to potential clients, and positioning yourself as an expert in your industry. As we delve into the power of networking and its role in lead generation, we uncover the profound impact it can have on nurturing leads, forging valuable partnerships, and propelling your business into the forefront of your industry. Join us on this journey as we explore the essential strategies and tactics that harness the potential of networking and transform your business in the process.

- The Foundation of Lead Generation

Lead generation is the lifeblood of any business. It is the process of identifying and attracting potential customers, nurturing them through the sales funnel, and converting them into loyal clients. While various marketing techniques contribute to lead generation, networking stands out as a powerful, personalized approach that humanizes the sales process.

- ### Building Genuine Connections
Networking events, conferences, and industry gatherings create the perfect environment for professionals to come together, share insights, and build genuine connections. These interactions are not just about exchanging business cards or giving elevator pitches; they are about establishing rapport, understanding needs, and finding common ground. Building meaningful relationships based on trust and mutual interest lays the foundation for productive lead generation.

- ### The Art of Active Listening
One of the most underrated yet critical aspects of networking is active listening. When engaging with potential leads, the ability to listen attentively to their pain points, goals, and challenges enables you to tailor your pitch and solutions to precisely address their needs. Active listening fosters empathy and understanding, leading to a deeper connection with potential clients and increasing the likelihood of converting them into loyal customers.

- ### Positioning Yourself as an Expert
Networking provides a platform to showcase your expertise and position yourself as an industry thought leader. Whether through participating in panel discussions, giving presentations, or engaging in meaningful conversations, sharing your knowledge and insights sets you apart from the competition. As potential leads recognize your expertise, they are more likely to trust your products or services, making lead conversion more achievable.

- ### Get At Least 10,000 High-Quality and Tailored Leads a Month with ATS Leads
In the competitive landscape of business, finding the right leads that align with your target audience is crucial for sustained growth and success. That's where ATS Leads comes in – a leading expert in lead generation, harnessing the power of cutting-edge technologies and data-driven strategies to deliver results that propel your business to new heights.

Imagine leveraging Google's vast public database, social media platforms, targeted hashtags, and precise email lists to connect with your prospective clients. Our precision targeting ensures you discover customers who are not just interested but eager to buy from you. The possibilities are boundless, and the results are extraordinary.

Traveling with Trient

EXPLORING NEW HORIZONS:
UNLOCKING SAFE & AFFORDABLE TRAVEL ADVENTURES IN 2023

As the world slowly emerges from the challenges of the past, the allure of travel beckons like a distant melody, inviting us to explore new horizons and embark on thrilling adventures. After a prolonged period of restrictions and uncertainty, 2023 holds the promise of resuming our wanderlust with a fresh perspective and a newfound appreciation for the beauty that lies beyond our doorsteps.

However, in this new era of travel, safety and affordability take center stage. The desire to quench our wanderlust must be balanced with responsible choices that protect our well-being and financial security. Whether you're a seasoned globetrotter or a first-time traveler, mastering the art of safe and affordable travel in 2023 is essential for making the most of your journey.

RESEARCH, PLAN, AND ADAPT

THE KEY TO A SUCCESSFUL TRAVEL EXPERIENCE LIES IN PREPARATION. RESEARCH YOUR DESIRED DESTINATIONS, KEEPING AN EYE ON UPDATED TRAVEL ADVISORIES AND RESTRICTIONS. FLEXIBILITY IS PARAMOUNT, AS CIRCUMSTANCES MAY CHANGE AT SHORT NOTICE. EMBRACE THE ART OF ADAPTABILITY AND BE READY TO ADJUST YOUR PLANS IF NEEDED. UTILIZE ONLINE RESOURCES, READ TRAVELER REVIEWS, AND SEEK GUIDANCE FROM SEASONED TRAVELERS TO GAIN VALUABLE INSIGHTS THAT ENHANCE YOUR TRAVEL ITINERARY.

EMBRACE SUSTAINABLE AND ECO-FRIENDLY TRAVEL

AS WE EXPLORE NEW HORIZONS, LET'S BE MINDFUL OF THE IMPACT OUR TRAVELS HAVE ON THE ENVIRONMENT AND LOCAL COMMUNITIES. EMBRACE SUSTAINABLE TRAVEL PRACTICES, SUCH AS REDUCING PLASTIC WASTE, SUPPORTING ECO-FRIENDLY ACCOMMODATIONS, AND CHOOSING RESPONSIBLE TOUR OPERATORS. BY MAKING CONSCIOUS CHOICES, WE CAN CONTRIBUTE TO PRESERVING THE NATURAL BEAUTY AND CULTURAL HERITAGE OF OUR DESTINATIONS FOR GENERATIONS TO COME

STAY VIGILANT AND PRIORITIZE SAFETY

EVEN AS TRAVEL RESUMES, IT'S CRUCIAL TO REMAIN VIGILANT AND PRIORITIZE YOUR SAFETY. KEEP ABREAST OF HEALTH AND SAFETY GUIDELINES, PRACTICE GOOD HYGIENE HABITS, AND FOLLOW LOCAL REGULATIONS. TRAVEL WITH A WELL-STOCKED FIRST AID KIT AND BE PREPARED FOR UNEXPECTED SITUATIONS.

LEVERAGE TRAVEL TECHNOLOGY

IN THE DIGITAL AGE, TRAVEL TECHNOLOGY HAS BECOME AN INDISPENSABLE COMPANION FOR MODERN ADVENTURERS. FROM BOOKING FLIGHTS AND ACCOMMODATIONS TO ACCESSING REAL-TIME TRAVEL UPDATES AND NAVIGATION TOOLS, TRAVEL APPS AND PLATFORMS STREAMLINE THE TRAVEL EXPERIENCE AND ENSURE SEAMLESS JOURNEYS. EMBRACE TECHNOLOGY NOT ONLY FOR CONVENIENCE BUT ALSO FOR STAYING INFORMED ABOUT COVID-19 PROTOCOLS, SAFETY MEASURES, AND DESTINATION-SPECIFIC GUIDELINES.

INVEST IN TRAVEL INSURANCE

IN THE UNPREDICTABLE LANDSCAPE OF 2023, TRAVEL INSURANCE IS A WISE INVESTMENT. IT PROVIDES A SAFETY NET IN CASE OF UNFORESEEN EVENTS, OFFERING PROTECTION AGAINST TRIP CANCELLATIONS, MEDICAL EMERGENCIES, AND OTHER TRAVEL-RELATED RISKS. REVIEW DIFFERENT INSURANCE OPTIONS AND CHOOSE COVERAGE THAT ALIGNS WITH YOUR TRAVEL PLANS, ENSURING PEACE OF MIND THROUGHOUT YOUR JOURNEY.

EMBRACE THE OFF-SEASON

TRAVELING DURING THE OFF-SEASON NOT ONLY GUARANTEES FEWER CROWDS BUT OFTEN COMES WITH COST SAVINGS AS WELL. DESTINATIONS THAT EXPERIENCE PEAK SEASONS MAY OFFER MORE AFFORDABLE OPTIONS DURING QUIETER PERIODS, ALLOWING YOU TO EXPERIENCE THE ESSENCE OF A PLACE WITHOUT THE HUSTLE AND BUSTLE. ADDITIONALLY, OFF-SEASON TRAVEL CAN PROVIDE A UNIQUE PERSPECTIVE, AS YOU WITNESS DESTINATIONS IN A DIFFERENT LIGHT.

As we set out on our travel adventures in 2023, let's embrace the thrill of exploring new horizons while treading responsibly. By unlocking safe and affordable travel experiences, we can savor the beauty of the world around us while ensuring its preservation for generations to come. So, pack your bags, prepare your sense of wonder, and let the journey begin!

ANTONIO T. SMITH JR.

Pre-Order now

EXPLORING NEW HORIZONS:
TIPS FOR FINDING *Inspiration* IN TRAVEL

Successful Authors and Entrepreneurs: How Travel Inspired Their Stories

By: M.L. Ruscsak

Travel is a powerful catalyst for change, and for many successful authors and entrepreneurs, venturing into new territories has been the driving force behind transformative ideas and accomplishments. In this article, we'll delve into the journeys of two remarkable individuals whose globetrotting experiences have sparked change, innovation, and growth in their respective businesses and literary creations. From the rolling hills of Tuscany to the bustling streets of Tokyo, these adventurers have embraced the unknown, allowing the world to shape their stories and ventures in ways they could never have imagined.

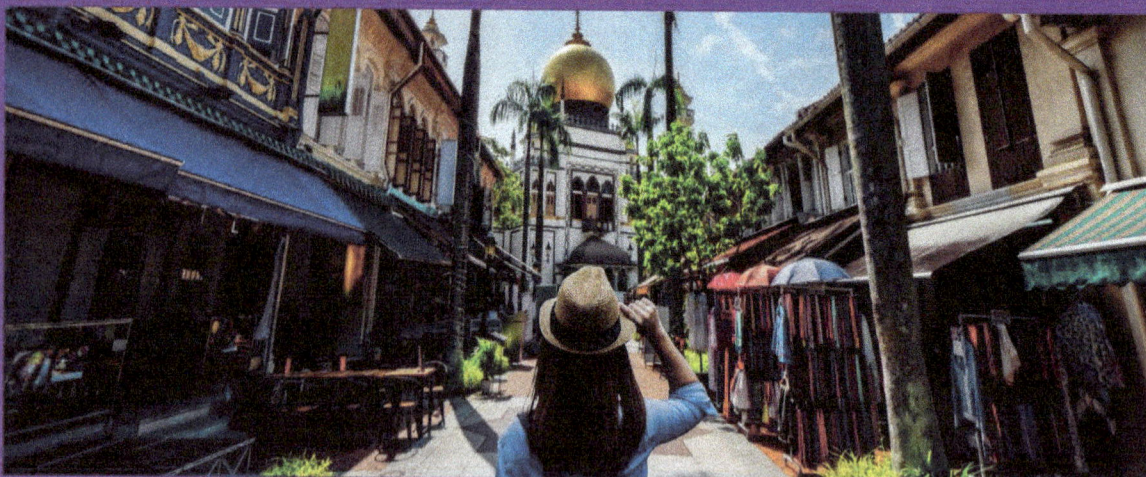

Elizabeth's Odyssey: Unraveling the World Through Literature

Elizabeth Connolly, a renowned author and avid traveler, has woven the tapestry of her literary masterpieces through her diverse travel experiences. From a young age, Elizabeth was captivated by the allure of foreign cultures, and her globetrotting pursuits have greatly influenced her writing.

In her first solo adventure to India, Elizabeth found herself immersed in a whirlwind of vibrant colors, captivating sounds, and the rich tapestry of life. This journey kindled her passion for storytelling, and upon her return, she channeled the essence of India into her debut novel, "Saffron Dreams." The book took readers on an evocative journey through the lives of characters who grappled with cultural identity and self-discovery, mirroring Elizabeth's own soul-searching experiences.

> *"The world is an exquisite mosaic of stories waiting to be unraveled. With each journey, I add another chapter to the book of my life."*
>
> *- Elizabeth Connolly*

Her travels didn't stop there. From the bustling streets of Cairo to the tranquil landscapes of Kyoto, Elizabeth's thirst for exploration breathed life into her subsequent novels, each a testament to the interconnectedness of the human experience.

Through travel, Elizabeth cultivated empathy, a deep understanding of diverse perspectives, and a boundless well of inspiration for her craft. As she continues her travels, she remains open to the magic of the world, eagerly awaiting the next chapter in her journey of literary discovery.

The Entrepreneurial Expedition of James Hudson

James Hudson, a trailblazing entrepreneur, attributes his professional success to the transformative impact of travel. As the founder of an innovative tech startup, James understands the importance of broadening horizons and seeking inspiration beyond the confines of the boardroom.

One defining trip that shaped James's entrepreneurial journey was a soul-searching expedition to the heart of the Amazon rainforest. Amidst the lush greenery and the symphony of wildlife, James experienced a moment of profound clarity that sparked the idea for his groundbreaking sustainability platform. This life-changing journey inspired him to build a company dedicated to fostering sustainable practices across industries, revolutionizing the way businesses approach environmental responsibility.

Moreover, James's extensive travels across continents exposed him to diverse market trends and consumer behaviors. In a bustling marketplace in Hong Kong, he observed the seamless integration of technology into everyday life, leading him to pivot his company's focus towards innovative mobile solutions. With each voyage, James gained invaluable insights that fueled the growth of his startup, propelling it into the forefront of its industry.

> *"When I set foot on foreign soil, I feel like an explorer venturing into uncharted territories. Every journey opens my mind to new possibilities and fuels my passion for innovation in business." - James Hudson*

Beyond business, James's travels have also influenced his approach to leadership and team dynamics. From learning the art of negotiation in bustling bazaars to embracing cultural nuances during international collaborations, James attributes his interpersonal skills to the global education he received while traveling.

For Elizabeth Connolly and James Hudson, travel has been the guiding compass leading them to remarkable achievements in the realms of literature and entrepreneurship. Their adventures have broadened their perspectives, infused their work with authenticity, and enriched their lives with unforgettable experiences. As the world continues to beckon, these successful individuals stand as a testament to the transformative power of travel, inspiring others to embrace the unknown and embark on journeys that could change the trajectory of their own stories.

EXPLORING THE SWEET ADVENTURES OF HERSHEY PARK AND IMMERSING IN HISTORY AT GETTYSBURG, PENNSYLVANIA

Nestled in the picturesque landscapes of Pennsylvania, a world of sweet delights and historical marvels awaits. Hershey Park and Gettysburg, two iconic destinations, beckon travelers with their unique allure and captivating experiences. For families seeking a perfect blend of fun, excitement, and learning, this delightful duo offers an unforgettable adventure. Join us as we embark on a journey to rediscover the charm of Hershey Park's chocolate paradise and delve into the rich historical tapestry of Gettysburg.

Part I:
Hershey Park - A Chocolaty Wonderland for All Ages

At Hershey Park, magic is infused with the irresistible aroma of cocoa. This chocolate-themed amusement park, located in Hershey, Pennsylvania, is a dream come true for kids and the young at heart. Founded by Milton S. Hershey, the visionary entrepreneur behind the world-famous Hershey's chocolate, the park continues to be a testament to his sweet legacy.

Hershey's Chocolate World: Kickstart your adventure with a visit to Hershey's Chocolate World, the gateway to the whimsical world of chocolate. Here, you can take a delightful tour to learn about the chocolate-making process, create your personalized candy bar, and even meet the beloved Hershey's characters.

Thrilling Rides and Entertainment: Hershey Park boasts an array of exhilarating rides for thrill-seekers, ranging from heart-pounding roller coasters to family-friendly attractions. Feel the adrenaline rush on iconic rides like Fahrenheit and Skyrush, or embark on a nostalgic journey with the historic Comet coaster. The park also offers captivating shows and entertainment for moments of relaxation and delight.

Water Park Adventures: Beat the summer heat at The Boardwalk, Hershey Park's water park, featuring refreshing water attractions and wave pools. From thrilling water slides to lazy river rides, there's no shortage of water-based fun.

Part II: Gettysburg - Stepping into the Pages of History

A short drive from Hershey Park, Gettysburg awaits with its profound historical significance and enchanting charm. This small town holds a pivotal place in American history as the site of the eponymous Battle of Gettysburg during the Civil War.

Gettysburg National Military Park: Immerse yourself in history as you explore the hallowed grounds of Gettysburg National Military Park. Walk in the footsteps of soldiers who fought valiantly during the three-day battle that changed the course of the Civil War. The park offers informative guided tours and a visitor center with fascinating exhibits that bring the past to life.

Historic Downtown Gettysburg: Stroll through the quaint streets of downtown Gettysburg, lined with charming boutiques, art galleries, and restaurants. The town's rich heritage is evident in its well-preserved architecture and unique shops, offering a perfect blend of history and contemporary delights.

Haunted Tales and Ghost Tours: As the sun sets, Gettysburg's historic sites take on an eerie allure. For those who seek spine-chilling thrills, consider joining a ghost tour to hear haunting tales of the past and explore the town's paranormal mysteries.

Conclusion:

A journey to Hershey Park and Gettysburg is more than just a vacation; it's an experience that lingers in the hearts of families for years to come. Whether indulging in the sweet wonders of Hershey's Chocolate World or discovering the profound history of Gettysburg, these two iconic destinations cater to all ages and interests. So, pack your bags, gather your loved ones, and prepare for a delightful adventure filled with laughter, learning, and cherished memories in the heart of Pennsylvania.

THE HOTEL HERSHEY: A SWEET HAVEN OF ELEGANCE AND ADVENTURE

Nestled in the heart of Hershey, Pennsylvania, The Hotel Hershey offers a world-class experience that combines luxury, recreation, and indulgence. With 276 rooms, each exuding elegance and full-service amenities, this iconic resort promises a stay that is nothing short of exceptional.

Whether you choose a spacious guest room, a lavish suite, or a charming cottage, you'll be treated to the utmost comfort and hospitality throughout your visit.

Explore the Sweetest Destination On Earth:

When you step outside The Hotel Hershey, you'll find yourself immersed in a world of endless excitement and entertainment. Hershey, lovingly known as The Sweetest Place On Earth, lives up to its reputation with a myriad of attractions and activities to suit every taste. Experience the thrill of roller coasters at Hersheypark, cheer on your favorite hockey team at the Giant Center, or groove to live concerts under the stars. From family-friendly fun to thrilling adventures, Hershey leaves no room for boredom.

Revel in Recreation and Relaxation:

Within the hotel's elegant confines, guests can find respite and rejuvenation at every turn. Take a refreshing dip in the indoor pool, maintain your fitness routine at the state-of-the-art fitness center, or engage in friendly competition at the outdoor sports complex. The options for recreation are as diverse as they are delightful, ensuring everyone can find their perfect getaway.

Indulge in Award-Winning Dining:

Prepare your taste buds for a culinary journey like no other at The Hotel Hershey's six exquisite restaurants. From delectable dishes crafted with fresh flavors to elegant settings that exude sophistication, every dining experience is a celebration of the senses. Savor each bite, sip on exceptional wines, and immerse yourself in a world of culinary excellence.

Celebrate Your Dreams:

The Hotel Hershey is more than just a luxurious escape; it's the ideal venue for unforgettable celebrations. Whether you're planning a dream wedding or commemorating a special milestone, the enchanting ambiance of Hershey sets the stage for magical moments. Let your love story unfold against a backdrop of beauty, romance, and timeless elegance, and create memories that will be cherished forever.

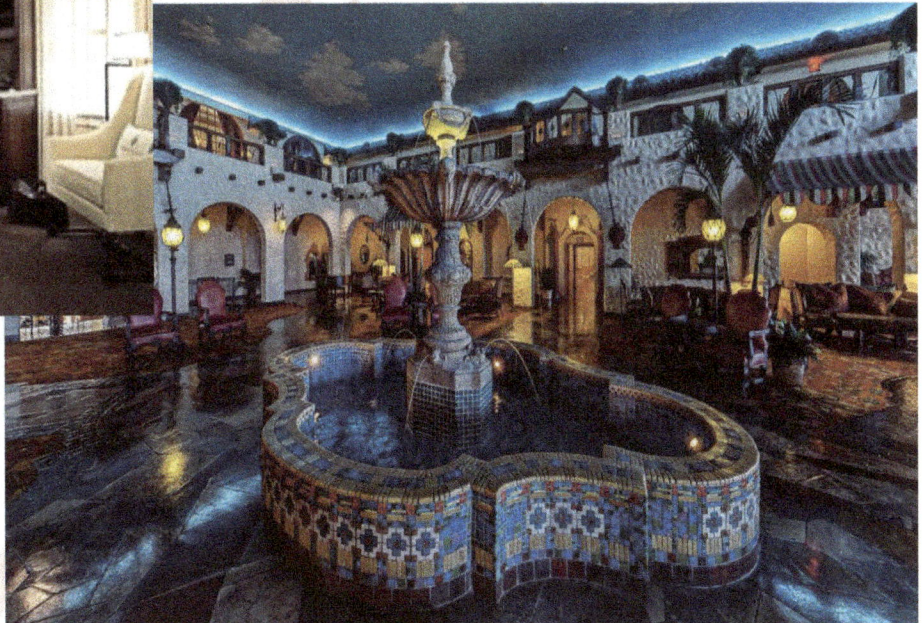

In conclusion, the Hotel Hershey is not just a destination; it's an experience that promises to awaken your senses and rejuvenate your soul. From the moment you arrive, you'll be embraced by a world of luxury, adventure, and indulgence, making every moment extraordinary. Embrace the sweet allure of Hershey, The Sweetest Place On Earth, and revel in a getaway that transcends the ordinary. Whether you're seeking relaxation, family fun, or a romantic escape, The Hotel Hershey awaits with open arms, ready to make your dreams come true in the most delightful way imaginable.

Navigating Company Leadership: A Tale of Two COOs - Pre and Post AI

BY: KRISTINA WENZL-FIGUEROA, VP & COO
TRIENNIUM LYONS MEDIA, TRIENT PRESS, LYTRIONS FILM

I n the intricate tapestry of running a company, the role of the Chief Operating Officer (COO) stands as a linchpin for operational success. But the story of two COOs, each navigating the ever-shifting landscape of business, reveals a stark contrast - the integration of artificial intelligence (AI). Embark on a journey as we dive deep into the personal narratives of COOs who treaded paths without and with AI, unearthing the profound impact AI has on operational efficiency and leadership.

Part I: The Era of Intuition - COO Sarah's Odyssey Without AI

Step into the shoes of Sarah, a tenacious COO who led a manufacturing company in the early 2000s. Her office buzzed with energy, but behind the scenes, her challenges were palpable:

Intuition in a Data Desert: Sarah was a beacon of intuition, her experience guiding her choices. But lacking real-time data insights, her decisions were rooted in gut feeling alone. She yearned for the ability to augment her instincts with concrete information.

Battling Midnight Fires: Predictive insights were a missing puzzle piece in Sarah's toolkit. The absence of these insights resulted in her scrambling to put out fires, often dealing with issues that had already escalated. She wished for the power to anticipate problems before they became crises.

Balancing Act in the Dark: Resource allocation was a tightrope walk for Sarah. Without AI's guiding hand, she often

grappled with uncertainty, struggling to strike the right balance between personnel, finances, and assets. She longed for a reliable compass to optimize her company's resources.

Drowning in Reactive Risks: Risk management felt like treading water in turbulent seas for Sarah. Without AI's foresight, she navigated uncertainties without a clear map, dealing with risks reactively rather than proactively. She dreamed of a way to predict and prevent potential pitfalls.

Stuck in Time: Market fluctuations were a challenge for Sarah's operations. The lack of agility left her company stuck in a time warp, unable to adapt swiftly to changing market dynamics. She envisioned a future where her operations could pivot with grace and seize opportunities.

Part II: The AI-Infused Expedition - COO Alex's Odyssey With AI

Zoom to the present and meet Alex, an enterprising COO steering a tech-driven conglomerate. Alex's journey is a symphony of innovation, orchestrated by AI:

Humanity Meets Data: Alex's leadership harmonizes human intuition with AI's real-time insights. This dynamic duo empowers Alex to make decisions grounded in data, enriched by experience, and deeply informed.

Anticipating the Storm: AI's predictive prowess empowers Alex to proactively anticipate and address bottlenecks. This proactive approach ensures that the company stays ahead of potential challenges and keeps operations on track.

Optimization Perfected: Resource allocation becomes a masterpiece as AI's algorithms gracefully orchestrate personnel, funds, and assets. The delicate dance of optimization is guided by data-driven precision.

Crafting Proactive Strategies: With AI's foresight, Alex's risk management playbook transforms from a reactive manual to a proactive guide. Potential issues are spotted in advance, and strategies are crafted to mitigate them before they escalate.

Mastering the Art of Agility: AI-driven automation gives Alex's team the tools to adapt swiftly, capturing opportunities and sidestepping threats. The company's ability to pivot becomes a true competitive advantage.

Tailored Excellence: AI-fueled insights enable Alex to tailor customer experiences, building relationships that extend beyond transactions. Each interaction is personalized, fostering lasting engagement and loyalty.

Navigating Uncharted Waters: With AI at the helm of routine tasks, Alex steers the company into innovative territories. Freed from the mundane, Alex embraces the role of a visionary, leading the company into uncharted horizons.

Transforming Publishing and Filmmaking with AI:
As the Vice-President and COO of Triennium Lyons Media, Trient Press, and Lytrions Film, I've lived through this transformation, reshaping the narrative of both publishing and filmmaking:

AI in Book Publishing: At Trient Press, AI-powered analytics unearthed niche markets for our authors, increasing revenue by 25% through targeted book releases. We transformed from relying solely on author intuition to data-backed strategies.

Streamlined Productions: AI's real-time insights at Lytrions Film allowed us to optimize production schedules, cutting lead times by 40%. This newfound agility resulted in faster deliveries and enhanced client satisfaction.

Enhanced Filmmaking: AI's capabilities at Lytrions Film have streamlined pre-production tasks, allowing for more efficient script analysis, casting decisions, and budget estimations. The creative process has been enriched by data-driven insights.

Risk Mitigation: AI-driven predictive analytics identified potential production delays at Trient Press and Lytrions Film, enabling us to take preemptive measures and ensure timely deliveries. We moved from crisis management to proactive planning.

Enhanced Author and Filmmaker Engagement: AI-fueled insights helped us tailor marketing strategies at Triennium Lyons Media, driving higher engagement and loyalty from authors and filmmakers. Our interactions are now more meaningful, resonating on a personal level.

To summarize, my story and those of Sarah and Alex illuminate the seismic shift AI has ushered into the COO realm, especially within the realms of publishing and filmmaking. It's the evolution from intuition-led management to AI-infused leadership. AI molds COOs into strategists, armed with both data and gut instincts, steering operational excellence, risk foresight, and inventive progress. The evolving AI landscape presents COOs with a unique choice – to harness AI's might and pave a trail toward efficiency or continue along the well-trodden path of yesteryears. It's a journey where decisions weave the fabric of tomorrow's leadership, bridging the gap between human insight and technological innovation, and giving birth to new possibilities in publishing, filmmaking, and beyond.

Hershey-Inspired Sweet and Savory Chocolate Glazed Chicken

INGREDIENTS

8 SERVINGS

- 4 BONELESS, SKINLESS CHICKEN BREASTS
- 1/2 CUP DARK CHOCOLATE CHIPS (70% COCOA OR HIGHER)
- 2 TABLESPOONS HONEY
- 2 TABLESPOONS SOY SAUCE
- 1 TABLESPOON BALSAMIC VINEGAR
- 2 CLOVES GARLIC, MINCED
- 1 TEASPOON DRIED THYME
- 1 TEASPOON DRIED ROSEMARY
- 1/2 TEASPOON CHILI POWDER
- SALT AND PEPPER TO TASTE
- FRESH ROSEMARY SPRIGS FOR GARNISH (OPTIONAL)

DIRECTIONS

- Preheat your oven to 375°F (190°C). Lightly grease a baking dish and set aside.
- In a small saucepan over low heat, melt the dark chocolate chips. Stir continuously to ensure the chocolate doesn't burn. Once melted, remove the saucepan from the heat.
- In a mixing bowl, combine the melted chocolate, honey, soy sauce, balsamic vinegar, minced garlic, dried thyme, dried rosemary, and chili powder. Mix well until all the ingredients are fully incorporated, and you have a smooth and velvety chocolate glaze.
- Season the chicken breasts with salt and pepper to taste. Lay them in the prepared baking dish, making sure they're evenly spaced.
- Pour the chocolate glaze over the chicken breasts, ensuring they are fully coated with the savory sweetness.
- Cover the baking dish with aluminum foil and bake in the preheated oven for about 20-25 minutes or until the chicken is cooked through, and the glaze has caramelized into a rich, glossy coating.
- Remove the foil and continue baking for an additional 5-7 minutes to give the chicken a nice golden color and added crispness.
- Once the chicken is done, remove it from the oven and let it rest for a couple of minutes.
- Serve the Sweet and Savory Chocolate Glazed Chicken on a platter, garnished with fresh rosemary sprigs for an extra touch of elegance.

DECADENT CHOCOLATE LAVA CAKES WITH RASPBERRY COULIS

Ingredients

For the Raspberry Coulis:
- 1 cup fresh raspberries
- 2 tablespoons granulated sugar
- 1 tablespoon water
- 1 teaspoon fresh lemon juice

For the Chocolate Lava Cakes:
- 1/2 cup (1 stick) unsalted butter
- 4 ounces Hershey's dark chocolate (70% cocoa or higher), coarsely chopped
- 1 cup powdered sugar
- 2 large eggs + 2 egg yolks
- 1 teaspoon pure vanilla extract
- 6 tablespoons all-purpose flour
- Pinch of salt
- Extra butter and cocoa powder for greasing and dusting the ramekins

Directions

For the Chocolate Lava Cakes:
- Preheat your oven to 425°F (220°C). Grease six ramekins with butter and dust them with cocoa powder to prevent sticking.
- In a microwave-safe bowl, melt the butter and chopped dark chocolate together. Heat in 30-second intervals, stirring in between until fully melted and smooth.
- In a separate mixing bowl, whisk together the powdered sugar, eggs, egg yolks, and vanilla extract until well combined.
- Slowly pour the melted chocolate mixture into the egg mixture, stirring continuously until the batter is smooth and glossy.
- Gently fold in the all-purpose flour and a pinch of salt until just incorporated, being careful not to overmix.
- Divide the batter evenly among the prepared ramekins, filling them about three-quarters full.
- Bake the lava cakes in the preheated oven for 12-14 minutes. The edges should be set, but the centers should still be slightly jiggly.

Directions (CONTINUED)

For the Chocolate Lava Cakes Continued:
- Remove the ramekins from the oven and let them cool for a minute. Then, run a knife around the edges to loosen the cakes. Carefully invert the ramekins onto serving plates to release the cakes.

For the Raspberry Coulis:
- In a small saucepan, combine the fresh raspberries, granulated sugar, water, and fresh lemon juice.
- Cook the mixture over medium heat, stirring occasionally, until the raspberries break down and the sauce thickens slightly. This should take about 5-7 minutes.
- Remove the saucepan from the heat and let the raspberry coulis cool for a few minutes.
- Strain the coulis through a fine-mesh sieve to remove any seeds, pressing down with a spoon to extract all the liquid.

To Serve:
Place a warm Chocolate Lava Cake in the center of a dessert plate, and drizzle the Raspberry Coulis over the top. Garnish with a few fresh raspberries for an extra burst of color and flavor.

The combination of the rich and gooey Chocolate Lava Cake with the tangy sweetness of the Raspberry Coulis creates a heavenly symphony of flavors, making it the perfect Hershey-inspired dessert to complete your unforgettable meal. Enjoy this delightful pairing that celebrates the essence of Hershey, Pennsylvania – the Sweetest Place On Earth!